Margaret Ann Logan

Sweet Alyssum

Poems

Margaret Ann Logan

Sweet Alyssum
Poems

ISBN/EAN: 9783744704779

Printed in Europe, USA, Canada, Australia, Japan

Cover: Foto ©Thomas Meinert / pixelio.de

More available books at **www.hansebooks.com**

SWEET ALYSSUM

POEMS

BY

MARGARET A. LOGAN

BUFFALO
CHARLES WELLS MOULTON
1894

CONTENTS.

SWEET ALYSSUM.

LOW border plant that forms such fair enclose
For our gay annual beds, or garden rows,
'Neath summer suns we view with calm delight
Thy tiny flowerets, honeyed tufts of white;
And in thy leaves' twas said there dwelt some power
To soothe the maddened soul.   A blessèd dower.

A DREAM IN THE DESERT.

(Abouasan, an aged Arabian, and Pharandaces, a young Persian, are on the road approaching an oasis).

PHARANDACES:

NAY, friend, I owned some charm in desert life
   At early morn, when yonder mountains threw
From their bald heads broad shadows to the base;
Or yester eve, when all the warm winds blew,
Moving the sand like some soft swell at sea.

ABOUASAN:

Ah! now 'tis changed indeed.

PHARANDACES:

Now, not the scant shade of o'er hanging rock;
And, here, the sand ridge-rolled as outcast field,
There, smooth as surf-beat shore or shingly beach,
That makes more tense this glare of quivering light.
Still, too, so still! No partridge heard to whirr,
Nor bark of jackal as he scours the plain,
No eagle flies its cloudland home to reach,
Only the vultures in broad circles sweep
Scenting the bones of some dead caravan.

ABOUASAN:

See here a crack in this straight ledge of rock.
It marks the entrance to some wady washed
By mountain stream.   Take heart! there's herbage
    near.

PHARANDACES:

And water, water, wherewith I may still
My patient dromedary's piteous moan.
I'll sponge his nostrils there, before I lave
My own sun-blistered lips, and give him fare
Other than camel-thorn ere I repose.

(*They enter the ravine and descend a few steps*).

ABOUASAN:

'Tis as we thought.   Behold green islands fringed
With arrowy rush!

PHARANDACES:

But water, where?

ABOUASAN:

Where grows yon royal palm amid the waste,
Rearing its head in lonely majesty.

PHARANDACES:

Voices I hear.   Right welcome company!

ABOUASAN:

This is the way that Sheba should return.
Some moons have waned since, westward, here she
    passed
Seeking the great king at Jerusalem.

PHARANDACES:

And didst thou see that wondrous train indeed,
And Yemen's queen, Balkis, the fair, the wise?

ABOUASAN:

A thousand odors filled the astonished air
Sickened so late by vulture's carrion breath.
Balsam and cinnamon, myrrh, frankincense,
And India's almug-tree their fragrance blent
While in the sunlight many a jewel shone,
With Ophir's gold.   And men, and camels all
In richest cloths were decked; finest e'er wrought
In India's famous looms, patterns most intricate
Such as thy country weaves.   And then the queen!

PHARANDACES:

Aye, Aye, the queen!

ABOUASAN:

Have patience, youth!   She mid her maidens rode
Like Persian pearl.   More bright than all the stones
That break the sunbeam in their lucid rounds.
Perfect she seems, from instep's high-arched curve,
To eyes soul lighted, whose unveiléd beams
Outshine Arcturus or Orion's band.
Proud stepped her camel, white, of Syrian breed,
Beneath her royal weight, and sweetly chimed
The silver bells that spanned his slender throat.

PHARANDACES:

In truth thou lovest the stars, and, loverlike,
Dost paint thy youthful queen, Abouasan.

ABOUASAN:

She is the daughter of our race and reigns
No less in Yemen's hearts than o'er its homes.

See there the tent upon the unbroken sward;
We will approach the men and share their salt.

(*While they are welcomed and refresh themselves,
the tent opens and the Queen of Sheba is seen con-
versing with Keturah, her favorite handmaid*).

KETURAH:

Then, thou wilt never wed?

BALKIS:

It may be, when more wisdom I have gained
Some fitting mate I shall consent to choose,
But love—speak not of that! For when there fell
Upon my brow the burden of a crown,
In that same hour I solemnly forswore
All selfish ties, all narrow household joys.

KETURAH:

I think my mother has the blame of this.

BALKIS:

My much-loved nurse! Of Hebrew lineage she,
And oft to us their legends would recount,
Rebecca's wooing thy most favored theme,
But I chose Miriam's triumphant song
Or Deborah's glorious chant of victory;
And then I longed to be a prophetess.

KETURAH:

So, when their great king's fame had reached thine
    ears,—

BALKIS:

I might not stay; but, maiden, speak no more,
Draw close the curtain. Let me rest awhile.

(*She sleeps, then starts up suddenly and calls her maids*).

BALKIS:

Oh! I have dreamed a dream, strange, beautiful!
Would that there were some learned Magi near.

KETURAH:

Abouasan and a fair Persian youth,
Pharandaces, are now within the camp.

BALKIS:

Haste; spread my carpets, I will sit without.

(*A throne is arranged beneath the palm and when
the strangers have been presented to the queen she
narrates her dream*).

BALKIS:

Alone, I was, amidst yon waste of sand
Weary my feet and scared with thirst my tongue;
I could have died with weariness and pain.
When, lo! a distant cloud, a caravan!
And, on a nearer view, they all were kings
That camels rode, white like my Syrian there;
Of every nation on this star-watched earth,
And weary seemed they as of hopeless quest.
Then came a voice, borne to me from within,
" A little Child shall lead them," and forthwith
A shout arose: "The Star! The Star! The Star!"
Loud was it echoed through that kingly throng.
In the clear sky of noon no sign appeared
And, yet, towards one point all eyes were bent;
'Twas in the west where the great temple stands.

Soon were they fled, for e'en the camels roused
From listless plodding stirred to gain that spot.
Then, but a western cloud, to me, appeared,
Far as the eastward, I had seen before.

ABOUASAN:

Strange dream, indeed!

BALKIS:

All not yet told, for as these onward moved
A mellow glow, such as our Yemen knows,
Displaced the fiery glare; and gently fell
A healing dew o'er all the parched ground,
So that the very thorns did bud and bloom
And bring forth full-blown roses, such as deck
Thy Persia's fairest plains, Pharandaces.

PHARANDACES:

A happy omen be thy beauteous dream,
And flowers e'er spring around thy royal way!

BALKIS:

Canst thou speak aught of this, Abouasan?

ABOUASAN:

Queen well-beloved, thou dost thy lineage trace
From Sheba, worshipper of yonder sun;
All happy stars presided at thy birth,
But wisdom's planet crowned thy horoscope!
I met the famous magi of our land
When, reading thence thy future, they foretold,
Thou shouldst all women far excel in this
The love of learning, and thy name should be
Through ages known as, Seeker of the truth.

(Keturah).

The Lord of hosts the conqueror of sin
Lift up your heads ye gates!

CHORUS.

Lift up your heads!   Lift up your heads!
Lift up your heads ye gates!

(Keturah).

Be ye lift up ye everlasting doors!

(Maidens).

And who is he that entrance now implores?

(Keturah).

The Prince of Peace whom heaven and earth adores.
Lift up your heads, ye gates!

CHORUS.

Lift up your heads! Lift up your heads!
Lift up your heads, ye gates!

BALKIS:

The Prince of Peace!   He cometh as a child;
The Lord of host, strong, mighty to prevail.
Oh! may he haste, indeed, to enter in
And bring the nation's wisdom, safety, peace.

(All join in the chorus until the very rocks resound).

Lift up your heads!   Lift up your heads!
Lift up your heads, ye gates!

BALKIS:

So have I heard, but this reads not my dream.

ABOUASAN:

Spake not the great king of Messiah's reign?

BALKIS:

Full oft, and in their sacred books 'tis said
Some Son of Solomon shall rule the world,
A greater yet than he.

ABOUASAN:

Wiser as child than he the wisest king;
Glorious with glory earth ne'er dreamed before;
Drawing the nations all with wondrous power,
Even as Solomon, by fame, hath drawn
Thee from thy home in Araby the Blest.

KETURAH:

And so thy memory of these Hebrew tales,
Yon oleander, bright as Sharon's rose,
And all the leagues thou didst so wearily
Tread through the burning sand—

BALKIS:

Nay! nay! some dreams be only fancies wove
From waking hours.   This, I believe
Was sent me by the stars.   Go, bring thy lute,
And maidens, sing that Temple song that speaks
The advent of some king.

(*Keturah sings*).

Lift up your heads ye gates!
The King of Glory waits to enter in.

(*Other maidens rejoin*).

Who is this king that waits to enter in?

THE LITTLE GREEN DRESS.

SOON will melt the ice and snow,
　　Soon the buds begin to blow,
And the birdies will be building as they sing;
　　Then a new dress made with care
　　Must my little girlie wear,
Fresh and fair is she as any flower of spring.

　　Come, my maidie, tell to me
　　Of what color it shall be,
White like daisies with their pale pink rim,
　　Or like the violets blue,
　　Or the yellow cups that strew
The bank beside the babbling brooklet's brim?

　　She will have a robe of green,
　　So declares my tiny queen.
Six springtimes has my little girlie known,
　　But last year she first, alas!
　　Watched the creeping of the grass
Until all the bare, brown earth was overgrown.

　　Then she thought that tender green,
　　Sweetest color she had seen;
So, green shall be the dress she is to wear.
　　To the town I soon must go,
　　Soon as melts the winter snow.
And a pretty gingham, green, I'll buy her there.

* 　　* 　　* 　　* 　　* 　　*

There's no flake of snow around;
　Frost and ice have left the ground;
Snow, frost and ice are all within my heart,
　For, before the daisies smiled,
　Death came and claimed my child;
And from me now, will winter ne'er depart.

There, within the orchard shade,
　They a tiny hillock made;
Then, quickly crept the grass and clothed it o'er,
　Clinging like a soft caress;
　And this was the green dress
The dress of green my precious baby wore.

Yet, sweet dreams will come to me;
　Oft, in visions, I can see
Wondrous light, and hear a wondrous song;
　Then my frozen heart will thaw,
　For in dreaming, thus, I saw
A white robed child amid a shining throng.

SUNRISE.

MID rugged hills before the break of day,
  A vale below, above, the mist-crowned height,
My roan and I had, darkling, picked our way
  'Till dawn's first glow shut in the stars of night.

Quick, then, began o'er mountain top to float,
  That field of mist. Here pale, there dark, it broke;
In wondrous forms, where on their outlines smote
  The hidden beam, touched with a light that spoke

Of lingering glory. Soon, those cloud-built forms
  Brought to my mind the sun-myths of all lands,
That vaguely mirror how our dear Lord rose,
  Shone the true Light, and loosened death's dark
    bands.

Majestic pillars now old Norse gods seem;
  In converse deep resolve they how to wake
Balder, the bright one; and yon dazzling gleam,
  Is wave of Siegfried's sword. With one wild shake

Of every fiery mane, far upward spring,
  Apollo's coursers, who drag in the day.
Here mounts Bellerophon; each heavenly wing,
  Pegasus spreads to bear him to the fray.

Where light with darkness strives, and find we there,
  England's St. George whose dragon dread lies
    slain,
Though from the carcass living heads uprear
  While he fights on and gives no stroke in vain.

A serpent coiled doth wake to sudden bound,
  My startled steed.   This brings me to the Nile,
The winged sun-disk this reptile twines around,
  Held sacred there, with us the type of guile.

Assyria next; Shamar at last has freed
  Ishtar the fair from all the powers of hell;
So through the nations runs the self-same creed.
  I wake from dreams at sound of chapel bell.

Of pealing bells.   For now the sun's first ray
  Gilds yonder village cross; it shines in scorn,
Of faiths less pure.   New flowers bloom on the way
  And birds sing blithely, " This is Easter Morn."

AT SUNSET TIME.

A T sunset time,
    Give me no noisy, bustling crowd around,
Give me no giddy mirth nor jarring sound;
For I would then be silent and alone,
Or with me take some friend whose spirit's tone
    In sympathy would chime.

    It matters not the clime;
Whether that glory linger on the crest
Of snow-wreathed hills, or, in soft blushes rest
On mountain lake, or from that splendor break
Clouds red and gold, the artist soul to wake
    Or gem the poet's rhyme.

    It whispers faith sublime
Of suns not lost, but rising on some shore
Unknown.   Of loved ones gone before.
Of endless dawn from shade of earth e'er free.
Let me not miss that message writ for me
    At sunset time!

ARIADNE.

'TWAS years ago, in Rome, I had this dream.
    'Mid its dark catacombs I groped, led by the
      gleam
From one pale torch held in my nervous grasp,
While closer still my right hand sought to clasp
The coil of string, that slender backward guide
To light and air.   Now, soon on every side

Strange sights I saw.   Such heaps of dead men's
    bones
And grinning skulls; I fancied dying groans
And visions saw of martyrs at the stake;
Reading some scrolls, I sudden turned to take
The path that once to an old chapel led,
There my foot slipped—and lost, my guiding thread!

Oh, agony! thus living chained to death!
I cursed and prayed, all in one quivering breath.
The skulls still grinned, they seemed to understand.
I groped and groped, but only grasped the sand.
The torch burned low as every path was tried;
Some low, some high, some narrow and some wide.

At last one led me to an open space
Where the old altar stood, and there a face,
An angel face from out the dim light shone.
And resting near it on the hallowed stone
Lay my lost thread.   Oh, joy, like a new birth!
Again to see the sun, and warm green earth!

Not all a dream.   In labyrinth as dire,
Of aims confused and uncontrolled desire,
I wandered long and seemed e'er doomed to grope;
No outward clue, lost to all higher hope;
Then shone the angel face, 'twas thine, my wife,
I found through thee the lost thread of my life!

THE FIRST FOOT.

A BONNIE lass at the ingle sits,
  The Old Year is almost dead;
Nimbly, as by the blaze she knits,
  Her needles throw off the thread.
The night is cold and the sky is dark,
  And the wind is wailing sore;
But 'tis New Year's Eve, and the maid must mark
  The first foot to cross her door.

"Rest, Jeanie, dear, for the hour is late:
  How the wind doth moan and sigh!"
"Mother, come knit beside me and wait
  Till we see the Old Year die.
My lover true will then come to me,
  My love from the Solway shore;
This word he has sent, that his own shall be
  The first-foot to cross my door."

"True, Jean, the auld wives say that ill
  Or good, for the coming year,
Will follow the one who o'er the sill
  First steps. But the night is drear.
He can never brave this wind and rain,
  So rest, now, and rise before
The day well dawns. When you listen again
  Your first foot may cross the door."

"Knit with me," still the maiden said—
  Together they watch and wait;

The cuckoo-clock sounds twelve o'erhead,
    And her lover is at the gate.
"Ah, now," cried Jean, "there's no ill to fear,
    Good luck is for us in store;
Since my lover has braved the night so drear,
    The first foot to cross our door."

BY THE OLD MILL.

MEET sovereign seemed she of that rural place,
For flower and stream had lent her every grace;
As the fair foam, her face and neck were pure.
Tho' each soft cheek the Azalia's blushes wore,
The jasmine's hue was in her flowing hair,
And many a playful sunbeam, sporting near,
Burnished its gold; her eyes of tender gray
Shone clearer than the water's crystal spray,
Sweet violets pressing forth her steps to greet
Less dainty seemed beside her dainty feet:
Some bird had taught her its melodious note,
For as I gazed, sweet strains began to float,
By gentle breezes borne the banks along,
And this, the burden of the maiden's song:

Ripple bright water, ripple and splash,
　Over the busy wheel;
Then to the greenwood merrily dash,
　Through ferny thickets steal;
Flow on, flow on, to the fay-queen's bower
　Under the hawthorn tree,
And ask of her elfin grace the power
　To bring a true lover to me;
To me, to me, to me,
　To bring a true lover to me.

For this is the merry month of May,
　A time when every bird
Is seeking to name its wedding day,
　Their wooings sweet I've heard;

E'en the cawing crow begins to coo
   Soft as the turtle-dove,
And I, with the birds, am waiting too,
   For some one to whisper love;
Love! love! love!
   For some one to whisper love!

She paused, and ere the strain so tender sweet
Died on the enchanted air, her tiny feet
Had left the mourning violets all alone,
And from my heart earth's brightness too had flown.

IN MEXICO.

I WANDERED to-night, in Mexico,
  While waiting for you; see, 'tis half past ten.
"And what did I find there?"
    Come, listen, then.
I saw those mountains that snow-crowned stand,
And the Aztec city—'twas not so grand
As Prescott paints—and the lakes around,
And I saw Cholula, that ancient mound.

I saw mesquite groves, lime and orange bowers,
Cacti, orchids and lilies, the rarest flowers;
Juan doffed his broidered sombrero,
And Juanita folded her mantle so
That her charms I guessed from one glimpse, alone;
Like stars through the dawn her dark eyes shone.

There were houses of stone with walls quite thick,
And others of adobe, a sundried brick.
I saw feather-work, and pearl-carvings rare,
Fire-opals and onyx; and sitting there,
I played at curveta, a gambling game
For women; our lotto is much the same.

I drank goat's milk and ate peppery meat,
Tamalis called, and then, nueces sweet,
Cheese made from the fruit of the prickly pear,
And tortillas, a bread they from corn prepare,

Soaked in water and lime and ground quite fine;
Then I took just a sip of Maguey wine,
That famous pulque.   A magic glass,
Scare drunk ere heroes began to pass.

I saw, by his men, Montezuma shot,
And Guatimozin tortured, yet murmuring not;
I witnessed their dread sacrificial feasts;
Saw Cortes, Las Casas, viceroys and priests;
"Remember the Alamo!" heard the Texans cry
As the Stars and Stripes swiftly floated by;

'Twas Taylor, and Quitman, and Twiggs and Scott,
Who bore them along, and they faltered not
Until gained were the heights of Chapultepec;
Then the Aztecs hastened their land to deck
For an Austrian prince who had come to reign;
Soon, soon did the star of his empire wane.

I saw him shot, and Carlotta's sigh,
Borne over the ocean, seemed wafted nigh.
That broke the spell, I was only here
Wondering at your lohg absence, dear,
And I smiled when I thought you'd be pleased to
        know
How I wandered to-night in Mexico.

"How did I get there?"   You heard the band
Playing to-night at their usual stand.
Strange! is it not? that a well-tuned string,
Or a tube well-voiced, has such power to bring
A spell o'er the wondrous realm of thought,
Until visions appear, uncalled, unsought,
And as fancy bids, we rove to and fro,
So, I wandered to-night in Mexico.

BLUE INNOCENTS.

GRAY in the sky, slow moving clouds of gray;
   Bare all the trees, save where in clusters clung
The forest vampire, gray-green mistletoe,
Or where the long gray moss in garlands swung
   From lofty limb to leaf-strewn walk below,
   By the wild winter wind tossed to and fro.

So weeks of gloom, then in a happier day
The red-bud dreamed of spring, and purpling,
    threw
   Its roseate boughs athwart the forest brown;
The gladsome sunbeams gave a silvery hue
   To the sad moss, and on the turfy down
   Houstonia came, its fairy knolls to crown.

Parting four petals, each a sapphire ray,
All set between with little golden eyes.
   'Tis well called Innocence, the dainty flower,
So like an infant, as it dreaming lies
   On mother's breast, waked by a sudden shower
   Of kisses soft and warm, the baby's dower.

THE RESURRECTION FLOWER.

NEAR that curst city compassed round
  By Israel's host, till at the sound
Of trumpet blast it fell;
I stood upon the shingly shore,
A western wind from Bethlehem bore
  The sound of convent bell.

Far distant, shone the sapphire sea,
But here, more welcome sight to me,
  The pearly Jordan rolled;
For, by its banks, the Son of God,
With human feet, had often trod
  In blessed days of old.

An Arab chief was resting near,
Wafting away the clouds of care
  In wreaths of fragrant smoke;
"Abu," I said, "what thinkest thou?
Is there a God?" With placid brow,
  The shiek his silence broke.

"My brother, truly hast thou said
There is a God," he bowed his head.
  "Abu, one question more—
Dost think that, though this body dies,
From dust it shall some day arise
  And live forevermore?"

Stooping from mid the herbage gray,
He drew a shapeless ball that lay
  Just at the river side;
A mass of leaves all curled and brown,
Like those that chilled by winter's frown,
  In some rude hollow hide.

Placing it where each rippling wave
The withered roots might gently lave,
  He said, "My brother, know,
Our Father's God, this truth hath showed
To Ishmael's sons, when He bestowed
  The Rose of Jericho!"

Its home it makes in desert sand,
There blooms and dies.   No human hand
  Removes that shrivelled coil,
But, o'er it sweeps the simoom strong
On wings of wind 'tis borne along
  'Till lodged in holy soil.

"Now let my brother mark the rose!"
We waited, day began to close,
  Longer the shadows grew;
And, o'er the slopes of Olivet,
The sun, as royally he set,
  Threw many a radiant hue.

Then, lo! the coilèd roots unwound,
Each tiny leaflet late embrowned,
  Soft living tints assumed;
And, like some corpse restored to breath,
Type of Christ's triumph over death,
  Anastatica bloomed!

OCTOBER.

KING'S messengers are now upon the hills,
 Their golden crowns amid the sunset gleam,
And all that crimson blaze that clouds we deem
Is trail of purple robes. Earth throbs and thrills
'Till a like splendor all the forest fills;
 And in the east the late wild roses seem
 Lingering to watch that glorious western beam,
Who comes? Who comes? Some conqueror dread
 who wills
With show of pomp to cloak the work of death?
 Nay, nay, 'the Lord our Righteousness,' his name;
 'Eternal Life,' his heralds all proclaim;
 This to his subjects he doth freely give.
"Live, live forever,"—hearken what he saith,—
 "Live, live forever; come to me and live."

ALEXANDER AND JADDUA.

THE Conquer comes! so rang the fearful cry
    Around Jerusalem.   Each encircling hill
Made mournful echo, and a shuddering sigh
    Swept through the olives of Gethsemane, until,
Filling each street, it hushed the city's hum—
He comes in wrath!   The Conqueror has come!

All through the day the temple courts were thronged
    With worshippers, and high the heavenward flame
Of sacrifice uprose, with prayer prolonged
    'Till midnight hours, yet no deliverance came—
God of our fathers! Israel's strength and stay!
Wilt Thou forsake us in this direful day ?

Grey morning dawned, and in their midst appeared
    The high priest Jaddua, who, with tears, had
        sought
Jehovah's guidance.   Gladly, he declared
    A heaven sent dream had this strange message
        brought:
" Go forth to meet the foe!   Wear robes of state!
Adorn the city!   Open wide each gate."

On came the mighty Macedonian host
    Which twice had overcome proud Persia's power;
Phenicians, Chaldeans, aye, those ranks might boast
    Each race had yielded them its martial flower; ·
The prospect place was reached, called Sapha, where
In after-years fell Jesus' pitying tear.

What wondrous sight there burst upon their gaze!
   A throng of people clothed in garments white,
And foremost Jaddua.   'Neath the noontide rays
   The golden plate upon his breast gleamed bright,
Showing God's name.   A purple robe he wore
And his broad brow the sacred mitre bore.

The Syrian kings, then, greatly joyed to see
   Those hated Jews; for, soon, like mighty Tyre,
Low in the dust Jerusalem would be.
   "Had not these people roused the conqueror's ire
When they refused the Persian oath to break
And a new league with Alexander make?"

Not long o'erjoyed, but angered and amazed
   When leaving them, the worshipped prince drew
      near,
Saluted Jaddua, on his breast plate gazed,
   And praised the Holy Name engraven there—
"Why shouldst thou, whom all the other men obey,
Unto this Jewish high priest homage pay?"

So questioned they, Parmenio at the head.
   "No priest I worship, but that gracious God
Whom he adores," then Alexander said,
   "For ere the soil of Asia I had trod,
"In Macedonia, still of doubtful mind,
"One came to me in vestments of this kind.

"'Twas in a dream, and thus the vision spake:
   "Make no delay, but pass beyond the sea;
"God destines thee Darius' power to break
   "And thou shalt conqueror of all Asia be.
"Now, when this priest in the same garb I view,
"Assured I feel the promise shall be true."

Back through the city gates all passed in peace
   And to the temple Alexander led
To offer sacrifice.   Jaddua, to increase
   His faith in heaven, there from the prophet read
How God had shown to Daniel, years before,
The four-winged leopard should the bear o'erthrow.

Then onward went the glorious young Greek,
   Nor blood, nor rapine only, marked his course;
Where'er he passed, still art and learning speak
   Of him who planted there their earliest source
So, like some prophet, he prepared a way
Where holy Paul should bear the Gospel ray.

THE WHITE ROBE.

"And they shall walk with me in white; for they are
worthy."—Rev. III, 4.

'TWAS winter, the earth lay brown and bare,
　　Save in snug little hollows here and there,
Green mosses and ferns were nestling near
　　Each crevice of clay or stone;
And on rising ground in the fallow field,
Stood holly and oak that are wont to wield
'Gainst the nipping frost a leathery shield,
　　Though the winds oft made them moan.

Other bushes and trees were leafless all,
For the life of the plant in early fall,
Fled back to the stem until spring should call
　　To each slumbering bud, "Appear?"
And the flowers, throwing their petals down,
Curled into the seed-pods dry and brown
And to visit the mother-root were gone,
　　Weaving clothes for their summer wear.

Then soft, still, slow,
Suddenly came the snow,
And lit the whole earth with unearthly glow;
Filling the hollows everywhere,
Hiding all that lay brown and bare,
And the greenest old oak was glad to share
This garment that shone so wondrous fair.

Soft, still, light,
It fell all through the night:
And the world that waked to the heavenly sight
Seemed to sleep and dream of that crystal sea,
Round the great white throne where the blessèd be,
Singing "Holy, Holy," eternally,
Clad in robes that are freed from every stain
In the blood of the Lamb that once was slain.

A multitude out of every land,
And the victor's palm is within each hand,
For their Captain there by the Judge doth stand
And his righteousness is the robe they wear.
Grant, dearest Lord, ere with souls made bare
Of earthly shams we shall each appear
Before that throne, on Thy Name we call
So that snowy robe may in mercy fall,
Hiding, cleansing and covering all;
Making us worthy to walk in white,
By the crystal sea in the Land of Light!

"UNDER THE BAOBAB."

THERE, 'neath the torrid skies,
Watched by no loving eyes
All that was mortal lies
Of Moffat's daughter;
Like a true, English wife
Shared she the toil and strife,
For souls gave her life,—
So love had brought her.

Where the Zambesi flows
Fed by the mountain snows,
There, then, her grave they chose;
Lianas now hide it,
Under that giant tree,
Noble old guardian he,
Scarce we the mound may see,
Rude cross beside it.

Thick grows the jungle grass,
Beasts from the river pass,
Only their cries, Alas!
Echoes there waken;
Yet doth the stream he found
Murmur with gentle sound
That humble home around,
Home, now forsaken.

Where they together wrought;
Livingstone healed and taught,
Sharing his task, she sought

Cares, all, to lighten.
'Till, through each tender vein,
Throbbed the fierce fever pain;
No more, might she remain
  Dark days to brighten.

Lone, then, he labored still
Sowing the Seed until
Glad, at the Master's will,
  Life he resigned.
Borne o'er the ocean wide
'Mid England's pomp and pride,
Hero and Saint beside,
  His dust enshrined.

Thus, though their ashes lie
Sundered the ocean by,
May meet their spirits nigh
  Afric's bright river,
Bending in blessing o'er
Those who, on that dark shore,
Toil as they toiled before,
  Souls to deliver.

Under the baobab tree
Where scarce the mound we see,
That woman's name shall be
  Murmured in blessing;
And, many a martyr band
Won from that heathen land
There, by her grave, shall stand,
  Christ's cross confessing.

TWO SPINNERS.

SLOW, slow, such endless toil
    With threads in an even row,
You spin so smooth, so soft, so fine.
Friend, let me show you a brave design.
    No answer?   Then off I'll go
And leave you to wind your simple coil,
Slow, slow, such endless toil!

Nimble and quick, angle and curve,
Spinning like mine doth praise deserve.
I draw out my thread, now low, now high,
And a web stands outlined against the sky;
Then I wait and watch, and 'tis not so long,
Ere is heard the hum of the insect throng.
Nimble and quick, angle and curve,
Spinning like mine doth praise deserve.

Well, ah! well, your work will stand
Until swept away by a careful hand.
The critic comes, you are fallen, crushed,
And that buzzing of praise is forever hushed.
Tis so when a spinner of cobwebs dies,
Naught but the end of his catching flies.

And how will my fellow craftsman fare
Who has wrapped himself in his cocoon there?
A glorious change that burial brings
For the toiling grub will have gained his wings,

And his work remains.   Reel off the floss,
Pure shining gold, not a sign of dross!
This gives one patience for working slow
With no pattern of brave design to show;
So I weave content, little cocoon mine,
Though the world is praising you cobweb fine.

SUCCESS.

I FANCIED her a fair and flower-crowned maid
   Compassed with rosy light,
And at her shrine youth, hope, and fortune laid;
   She never blessed my sight.

So passed the years, and I, grown old and gray,
   Thought not her wreath to wear,
For death had borne the loving friends away,
   Who joyed my joy to share.

'Twas then a calm-eyed, low-voiced woman came
   That dreary hour to bless.
I gently greeted and besought her name:
   Smiling, she said, "Success."

THROUGH LEAFLESS BOUGHS.

THE golden glories of yon beechen grove,
   Amid whose spreading boughs November
      strove
To hide in that bright veil the shafts of death
Flung with each falling of her frosty breath,
Lie in brown heaps or rustle o'er the plain
At wind's wild will, and branches bare remain!

Now stands revealed, a lovely glimpse of sky
The leafy screen had hidden from our eye,
Clear blue at noon; at even's earliest hour
Flushed with the soft pink of the almond flower,
And palest purple, such as violets show
Which in their native home mid mosses grow.

Dreams born of earth, fall with life's autumn day;
Some rudely break, some ripen to decay;
Through leafless boughs we look beyond and see
That home of light, that waits the soul set free;
Friends smile upon us who have passed before—
When such the gain, who would lost years deplore?

THE ORGAN.

I STOOD where all the nations of the earth
    Had gathered all their gifts, in the far South
By the great river's curve. And, there beheld
Sights such as make the old grow young once more
In spirit, freshened by the flood of ideas new
That come to swell the ebbing tide of thought;
The young grow old with glimpses of the vast,
Far-reaching field of knowledge spread before.
Sound, too, was there, all sound. The mighty roar
Of steam, the giant slave, who toils to-day
Like blinded Samson with his locks outgrown,
A people's sport and then a people's woe;
Mixed with the voice of man, the hum of wheels,
The chime of bells, and strains from Aztec land,
Played by her white-plumed band. Yet all seemed
    lost
In harmony that moment when the keys
Of the great organ, 'neath the master's touch
Sinking, set free the air in those great tubes,
And Mendelssohn, Beethoven, Mozart lived again
In heavenly symphony and wordless song.
While yet that echo lingered in my ears,
At home, I turned the German poet's page
And wove his legend into English rhyme.

      *   *   *   *   *   *

Cecilia was a maid of ancient Rome
Whose gentle heart, seemed framed for Music's
    home,

And long, she sought, from each vibrating string,
Those melodies to bring
That with unspoken rapture filled her saintly soul.
To her the faintest sound of living thing
In tuneful waves would roll.

Then sighing softly at devotion's hour,
Cecilia prayed sweet heaven would grant her power
To hear aright that wondrous song of praise
Which all the creatures raise,
A blessed angel who was hovering near,
Stooped, as he sped upon the Master's ways,
And smiling, touched her ear.
    Oh, ecstasy untold!
    As those once blind behold
    When first restored to sight
    Form lost in maze of light,
    So, with one mighty voice,
    She heard the earth rejoice;
    Heard living creatures all
    Upon each other call
    To magnify the Lord.
    Yet every tone was heard
    Of fish, or beast, or bird,
    The midge's tiny wing
    Its tribute come to bring,
    Faint rustling sounded o'er
    The lion's loudest roar.
    And though each sound was there
    Of earth, or sea, or air,
    Their burden was the same;
    "Praise ye the Lord and magnify his Name!"
    Great oaks and lofty pines,
    And graceful drooping vines,

The violet of the vale,
Queen lilies red and pale;
Nor sensate things alone,
For every clod and stone
Would sound a loved "Amen."
And grand the chorus when,
Strong wind and gentle breeze
Made harps of giant trees,
Waves dashed upon the shore
Waking a wild uproar.
Soft, sweet, slow,
Floating down below,
Down the celestial stairs
The music of the spheres
That poets oft have sung
In measured cadence rung.
The smallest orb that round the empyrean moved
Called on its sun to magnify the Lord.
No discord there, for even wrathful word
And groan of pain mixed with that strain was heard
But as a needed counternote to joy and praise,
Its perfect sweetness seeming yet to raise.
All must be harmony where all is tuned
To the great master-chord of Endless Love.

Too soon it died away, creation's song.
Then sought the maid the memory to prolong,
"Oh that the echo with us, yet, might stay !"
The heavenly herald heard her gently pray.
Then, one well-skilled in handiwork, he sought
Inspired like Bezaleel who wondrous wrought
In Sinai's wilderness, at God's command.
And lingering near him, led the willing hand

With reed and stop to fashion fittingly
A wondrous frame replete with harmony;
That every separate sound of earth, sea, air,
Might find some chord or note responsive there.

Again with praise all heaven and earth seemed
      stirred,
Again creation's song Cecilia heard.
" How shall I call this?" she enraptured cried—
The angel still stood smiling at her side—
"What name bestow on instrument so rare?"
"Call it," he said, "What thou didst seek in prayer,
Devotion's Organ. Let each soul express
Through this, its praise, its longing, its distress,
And that of other souls breathed through it hear
In sympathy. May never earth-bound spirit dare
To make these heaven-sent harmonies respond
To sound of base delight or pleasures fond."

            *   *   *   *   *   *

Cold, dead, that heart that at the organ peal
Can feel no holier impulse o'er it steal
To drown all earthly care,
Yet ne'er that heavenly echo comes to bless,
Filling the inmost soul with melody, unless
God's Angel touch our ear.

RIVER MURMURS.

MICHE Sepe! Prince of Rivers!
　　Flowing onward to the sea,
Though thy silver surface quivers,
　As the moonbeams dance with glee,
Those dark currents down below
Ever whisper words of woe!

From the lake that marks thy rising
　To the gulf that meets thy mouth,
From the northwest, enterprising,
　To the orange-blossomed South,
Men have come to make their graves
With De Soto and his braves.

Now reveal to me, great river,
　Tales of this and other days,
While I watch the moonbeam's quiver
　As it with thy ripple plays?
Hark! the river murmurs so,
Now of joy and now of woe!

THE REVENGE OF THE CRAY-FISH.

WHERE those lone live oaks are standing
   In that spreading sugar field,
Near the bank beside it landing
   Boats to bear the luscious yield,
Once was seen a planter's home,
Peering through their boughs, green dome.

With low roof but broad and shaded,
   Wide verandas all around
Which the mock-bird's song invaded,
   Symphony of sweetest sound;
In a garden gay with roses
Two fair children gathered posies.

When from all the fields were wending
   Loaded wains of sugared freight,
When the orange boughs were bending
   Burdened with a golden weight,
Busy hands while cutting canes
Sang their lively harvest strains.

Then two merry children playing
   By the river's muddy brim,
With pin-hook and line were slaying
   Such small fish as near it swim;
Shouting wildly with delight
When they took the fatal bite.

More than all the ugly cray-fish
    Was uplifted with applause,
For it furnished them a rare dish
    With its fat and juicy claws;
Better *bisque* than lobster gumbo,
Not these children only, thought so.

Soon the mill began its grinding
    And the carrier swift to run,
Then these careless playmates, finding
    Promise there of greater fun,
Left the cray-fish, now, to swim
Calmly near the river brim.

But while little lips were sipping
    The sweet cane juice running off,
And while little hands were dipping
    Cuite from out the cooling trough,
Vengeful cray-fish down below
Were swift swimming to and fro.

Spring is here! the bee is humming
    Wakened from his winter's rest,
And the swallow now is coming
    In the eaves to build his nest,
Sweet, the blooming orange trees,
Perfume every passing breeze.

List! the plough-boy's merry singing
    Chiming with the cattle bell,
And the children now are bringing
    Pale blue violets from the dell.
Coming home with glowing faces,
Breathing hard for running races.

Now the melted snow is making
    Torrent of each tiny stream
And the ice above is breaking
    'Neath the spell of warm sunbeam,
Then the unchained waters flow
Swelling that full tide below.

Soon the men are busy mending
    The high levee all around,
That their river-front defending
    Keeps the water within bound,
But those cray-fish down below
Still swim swiftly, to and fro.

And an old grandame is saying
    To the young fish at her side:
" While our enemies are playing
    We make entrance for the tide.
Many drills may sunder mountains,
Little holes can open fountains.

" Courage, then! with steady boring,
    By to-night, our work is done,
And the uncaged river, roaring,
    Shall, before another sun,
Bear those children on its waves,
Far beneath to watery graves! "

Night has come, the stars are beaming
    On two little golden heads,
And the children sweetly dreaming,
    Nestled in their downy beds:
Dreaming o'er their happy hours
Passed amid the birds and flowers.

Hark! what sound the stillness breaking,
　With a sudden gleam of light,
Those sweet sleepers rudely waking
　In the darkest hour of night?
Hear the dreaded signal pass.
This the cry, Crevasse! Crevasse!

Hear the frantic mother screaming:
　"Oh! my children! where are they?"
By the lantern's fitful gleaming,
　Little feet have lost their way,
And the waves, that fitful night
Bear them swiftly from her sight.

Gone, that happy home's foundation,
　Gone, the vines and orange trees:
On the spot, a cane plantation
　Overlooked by live-oak trees,
And beneath those currents deep,
Two fair children sweetly sleep!

THE STEAMBOAT RACE.

S PLENDID were those palace-packets,
    Ere the war between the states,
None though like that second Natchez
    And the Lee, those rival mates;
Bold the captains, clerks, and pilots,
    Famed for kindliest chivalrie,
But none loved like Thomas Leathers,
    And John Cannon of the Lee.

'Twas still June in Eighteen-seventy
    When both thronging stream and shore,
Were the eager waiting thousands.
    Signal scarcely given before
Swung the ax, her ropes were severed,
    And a well trained eye could see,
Though they seemed to start together,
    Gained two minutes had the Lee.

Now were men all betting heavy,
    While the women wildly waved,
Colored folk e'en risked their quarters,
    Children, dimes from candy saved;
And the rivals steamed by bravely
    ('Twas a glorious sight to see),
They had no freight, but passengers,
    Were forty on the Lee.

And among them walked one proudly,
    Like a millionaire just made,
For he held his shoulders squarely
    As some soldier on parade.
So we looked on him with wonder,
    But the cause soon learned when he
Came escorting a fair lady
    Up the cabin of the Lee.

Now this bride was tall and slender,
    Dark her coronal of hair,
Dainty mouth, and eyes that sparkled
    With a light so blue and clear
That it seemed like sunshine stolen
    From the cavern at Capri;
And we said, good luck came with her
    To the steamer Robert Lee.

When we swiftly steamed by Natchez,
    By fair Natchez on the hill,
All her citizens were cheering,
    Cheered for Leathers with a will;
But a group of small truck-farmers
    Had left plow in crop, to see,
And every coarse-clad veteran there
    Was hard betting on the Lee.

Then said some they greatly angered:
    "Will you go against the town?
Men, mark you not yon warrior
    With tomahawk and frown?"
And quick one answered, "Stranger,
    Yes, the figure-head I see,
And brave Injuns was them Natchez,
    But we fought with old Bob Lee."

Both made halt at war-worn Vicksburg,
  'Mid her terraces so green,
The loud guns roared out a welcome
  As those racers trim were seen,
Helping hands for both were ready,
  'Twas some test of fealty
Between their sister city Natchez
  And the loved old leader Lee.

We could rest no more till Memphis,
  With our rival still in sight,
On we sped, white wakes behind us,
  Like sea-meteors in the night.
Stopped the other to put coal on
  We towed coal along, you see;
Then good luck was ours; remember,
  For that bride was on the Lee.

So one hour ahead at Cairo,
  And still gaining on the way,
Until we reached St. Louis early
  Morn of Independence Day.
We had won, and loud they cheered us,
  But it gave no pain to see
When the Natchez made her entry,
  She had welcome like the Lee.

And they gave their city's freedom
  To each captain with his crew—
Some fair ladies have grown weary
  While I told this story true,
Of the last race on the river,
  (Such a race you ne'er will see),
Between Tom Leathers' second Natchez
  And her mate, the R. E. Lee.

ROCHE A DAVION.

IN that alcove scooped amid rising cliffs
   By nature's hand, safe float the skiffs;
There no rude winds blow, no wearing shock
Of beating waves against outstretched rock.
Ere white men claimed all this wide domain
And gained it often by deed of shame;
Here the Tunicas dwelt.   On yonder hill
Some stately trees spread their branches still;
Green as of old 'neath that grateful shade
Creeps the cheerful grass with its tender blade,
But their wigwam town that crowned its crest
Is forever gone.   Gone that symbol blest
Which once on the highest bluff appeared,
The cross of wood, Father Davion reared,

    *   *   *   *   *   *

Not for dreams of gold or fame, their home
Those Fathers left 'mid these wilds to roam.
The world was Christ's, so his name they bore
Through forests drear to a dreary shore.
Davion, the priest had his work begun
Amid the howling tribe of the sun
Whom we Natchez call.   They gave no heed
Too fierce and too proud for the gospel creed,
So he wandered here and a welcome found;
At eve would the Tunicas gather around
Filled with silent awe.   Then might be seen
Chief, papoose, and squaw, on the turfy green,

Stretched or standing erect while good Davion spoke
The message of peace from his pulpit-oak.
Their savage souls with soft wonder stirred
Would melt and glow 'neath that heavenly word.
"Now," cried the faithful Father aloud,
"Come confess and live who are contrite bowed;"
To the shore near that frienely alcove led
While the star of eve its faint lustre shed
And the deep dark river more calmly flowed;
There the sacred rite he, with prayer, bestowed.

     *   *   *   *   *   *

So years had passed when one morn was heard
No sound of prayer, and no voice conferred
The blessing of peace.   There was Davion where
So oft he had knelt, hands clasped in prayer,
His hair in the sun gleamed silver white
But the set face shone with a heavenly light.
They laid him to rest near his own loved oak
And long years after, old chieftains spoke
Of the good White Father in tones of awe
To the wondering youth.   Then the wrinkled squaw
Would her grandchildren often of Davion tell
How he prayed for the sick and could make them
       well
How his voice and his smile like new maize were
       sweet,
How for days he ate nothing, no bread, no meat;
And his spirit, they said, roved the old camp ground
Where no wigwam ruin could now be found;
When they saw it with hands as in blessing spread
All the tribe knew, then, that some chief was dead.

THE BROKEN ARROWS.

"GIVE us time our crops to harvest,"
   This the conquered Natchez pleaded,
" Ere we go new homes to make us."
   But their prayer was all unheeded;
One moon only gave the white men,
" Twenty days, and onward march then."

So, out spake the chief, White Apple,
   " We have borne but bear no longer,
Gone our homes, now would they starve us,
   Those false white men, nay, but stronger
Make our cause, oh, Great-Sun children!
Call we on our brave red brethren."

Swift then sped those Indian runners,
   Sought the Chickasaws and Choctaws,
Of the Frenchman's falseness told them,
   Bade all rise in one great Race-cause;
Quiver gave each tribe as token,
Twenty arrows, to be broken.

One each morning, this the signal,
   This the hour for joint uprising,
On that day when in each quiver
   No whole arrow.   Thus surprising,
All those white men they would slaughter.
Not so thought White Apple's daughter.

From the fortress twelve miles southward
   Stood her father's tribal village,
Fairest spot among the Natchez,
   Made more fair by care and tillage.
There the young braves met most often
For Stel-o-na's charms might soften

Heart most savage.   Stood those wigwams
   On the hillside, groves behind them
Of the walnut, oak, magnolia,
   'Mid whose branches wild vines twined them.
Round it ran a laughing clear creek;
Fair the maid those braves would there seek.

Like ripe chestnut-burr just bursting,
   Shone her bright eye neath its lid;
Sweet her presence as the pine-grove
   When dim twilight day has hid;
No vine rivalled her in wild grace,
Must she love the treacherous pale-face?

Said De Mace, the girl's French lover,
   " Twenty days your chiefs are granted
Ere they leave their happy homesteads
   Crops that their own hands have planted."
" Twenty days," she answered sighing,
" Then will white men all be dying."

So she gave him the dread secret,
   But they heard with scorn his story,
Placed the young man in confinement.
   Blind those Frenchman with vain glory,
To the temple then, at midnight,
Stole Stel-o-na through the moonlight,

Passed the guard who never hailed her,
  For he knew the chieftain's daughter
Though her long dark hair well veiled her,
  Cared he not what errand brought her.
From the roof, the painted eagles
Stared like three blood-thirsty beagles.

Passed the enclosing fence of pickets,
  From each stake a skull was grinning,
Skulls of foemen slain in conflict;
  Thus the maid, her entrance winning,
Stood beside the fire undying
Where those fatal arrows were lying.

Few were left, for onward marching
  Those brave allies to assist them;
Should these come the others joining,
  Vain were white men to resist them;
Arrows twain, in haste then taking,
Broke the maid; thus earlier making

For her tribe the bloody signal.
  So, before their friends could reach them
By swift march, they rose in conflict,
  Rose on those white men to teach them
How the Natchez now were stronger,
Much had borne, would bear no longer.

Slain then many a gallant Frenchman
  Ere the danger they discover,
Slain De Mace, and true Stel-o-na
  Perished there with her French lover.
But the Natchez power was broken,
False were their allies to the token!

A CHEROKEE ROSE.

THIS morn there opened in yon close-grown
        hedge
Of glossy green, that 'mid brown fields of sedge
    And barren boughs through winter gave us cheer,
Five heart-shaped petals, cream-laid, white as snow;
Wide ope'd that the large golden eye might show,
    As our field daisies shine when skies are clear.

Pure pointed buds pierced the encircling green,
The tender violets bowed as to their queen,
    Bright jasmine gaily yellow love knots tied;
And from the gulf a breeze bore fragrance sweet,
Tribute of orange groves, wherewith to greet,
    This Cherokee, we name Sequoyah's bride.

Forgot the chief? Nay, where cold glaciers gleam
Far up the snow-clad height, whose mountain
        stream,
    With roaring torrent, dashes in wild glee,
Its crystal spray to meet the pale green dome
Of feathery boughs.   There in its fitting home,
    See the Sequoia, giant redwood tree!

Far fitter this, than carved and fretted stone,
His memory to enshrine who toiled alone,
    From savage, warlike aims the tribe to free,
Letters he gave them, whence spread learning's ray,
Home-love and arts of peace until this day.
Noblest of Red men now, the Cherokee.

SOEUR MARGUERITE.

PERHAPS you remember Soeur Marguerite?
 She has gone to the saints and the virgin blest,
Whom she served so well, for there ne'er confessed
A purer soul, Pere Antoine would say,
When at matins and vespers she knelt to pray.
Ah! we knew her then but as maiden sweet,
Like our Lady of Sorrows grew Marguerite.

The orphan was placed at our convent when
Her aunt went abroad, and her home was there
For seven long years. 'Neath the tender care
Of the Sacred Heart and its sisterhood
Marguerite studied and grew both wise and good,
But untaught in the ways and wiles of men;
For of what avail was such knowledge then?

A learnéd maid and right skilled was she,
Could from memory say near her missal through,
And the life of each blessed saint she knew;
Of noted events would right dates declare,
Talked of places and products everywhere;
Three languages spoke with great fluency,
But the dear child's forte was embroidery.

Why, the flowers would grow as 'neath midday sun
When her little white fingers her needle drew,
In satin or cross stitch the canvas through!
She made finest lace, and would darn so well
That the keenest eye scarce a flaw could tell.
Oft would say: "When my school girl life is done,
I will take the vows and live here, a nun."

On her fête day Marguerite was seventeen,
Then the uncle and aunt all at once appear;
They will take her their city home to share.
She wept and she prayed: "Let me soon return."
But the guardians, angered her wish to learn,
Said they soon would the child from such folly wean,
When she New Orleans with its life had seen.

But her love for the Sacred Heart was strong.
Marguerite ne'er failed, 'mid that life so gay,
To send us a letter on every sixth day.
Opera music was grand, and she loved to dance,
But still felt too shy at the stranger's glance;
Some novels she read, and—was it so wrong?
For a love of her own she began to long.

To St. Roch's she walked the right number of days,
In his ivy-grown chapel her candle had burned,
Bought a little St. Joseph.   Then soon we learned
What she wished for had come—not one lover, but
        ten.
And she all untaught in the follies of men,
With their flattering tongues and their worldly-wise
        ways,
Would accept as a truth each light word of praise.

And the one that she chose in true worth was least,
But handsome and gay, and his suit so bold
That the innocent maid could not long be cold.
He was clever and rich, so both guardians bent
An approving smile when they sought consent.
We sent her a wreath that the dear old priest
Had blessed. They left home, and all tidings ceased.

When fourteen years passed, to the gate there came
A woman pale, sad, whom no sister knew.
Her hair was gray, but the eyes so blue
Were large and clear.   Then one, entering, said:
" This is Marguerite, we have mourned as dead."
And at once we saw that sweet soul the same,
Through the sunken cheek and the shrinking frame.

Her husband had ways that no wife could brook,
So she left him alone to his wine and his play,
And their only child he had stolen away.
Search in vain for her daughter, both far and near.
So the mother at last sought a refuge here;
She lived with us then, and the vows soon took—
You remember her eager, questioning look?

'Tis strange, she would gaze the most earnestly
At each girl that seemed near the age of ten,
Though some sixteen years was her daughter then,
Friends gave their aid, we renewed the quest,
And found her at last, holy saints be blessed!
Yonder fair-haired, blue-eyed girl you see,
- Please the Virgin, a nun shall this Marguerite be.

THE JOGGLING-BOARD.

YOUR terraced town by Centennial Lake,*
  "City"—beg pardon, friend,
I like full well, though one's breath 'twill take
  Just climbing from end to end.
In street or home, I have nothing seen,
  With such pleasant memories stored,
As yon well kept lawn, so smooth and green,
  And that bright red joggling board.

My childhood's friend! In infant days,
  A cradle, where soon and late,
Maum' Sabra sat singing quaint old lays,
  In the dear Palmetto State;
Then, in after years, young playmates came
  When the board would bend and spring,
With a joyous bound 'neath each childish frame,
  Our shouts made the echoes ring.

There was one, a girl. She only nine,
  While I was "going-on" ten,
Whose seat somehow was oft nearest mine,
  And, as often, it happened when
For greater fun all agreed to stand,
  Not easy to balance so,
I would seize and keep my neighbor's hand,
  And she never murmured "No."

A college lad, then, abroad I roam
  To return a S. T. B.
And the sweetest vision of coming home
  Was that neighbor I longed to see.
I found her, my simple blue-eyed girl,
  The belle of our native town.
When I left she gave me a golden curl,
  Now, her hair was chestnut brown.

One evening, eager to learn my fate,
  I paused at the gate and said,
" Shall we take a draft at the old well, Kate,
  For the sake of days that are fled ? "
Soft she answered, " Yes." No cup we brought,
  Naught so sweet as the good, old gourd;
All yet unsaid, then—happy thought—
  " Let us sit on the joggling-board."

For there it stood, and right down we sat,
  But no joggle, no hand in hand;
She, demure and distant; I, finding that
  Not a word could my voice command.
It was Kate herself, who the silence broke
  With some thought of the childish days.
Her tone was sad.   Then I quickly spoke,
  " Oh, could we thus stand always!

" As we stood in the happy days of old,
  My hand still clasping yours,
And joggle through life "—when once 'tis told
  How the heart all its love outpours!
A gentle start and an awkward spring
  From the board—you suppose she fell?
Why, what should a man then do but fling
  His right arm around her?   Well,

You know the rest, for you've seen my wife.
    Is not Tom a splendid boy?
Young man, there is nothing like married life—
    He's so pleased with that new toy—
Our girl will be ten the coming year,
    Like her mother with youth restored,
She is coming at last; see, Kate, my dear,
    Here's a genuine joggling-board!

THE CHINA TREE.

A MID the groves of our Southern land,
 More broad to spread and more firm to stand
 And fairer of form we see,
Magnolia shining with chaliced bloom,
Green oak and grave cypress, type of gloom,
 But I'll sing the China Tree.

When the settler comes and a clearing makes,
He smooths the ground and he drives his stakes
 Where the future abode must be;
But before a plank of the floor be laid
He will plant all around, for a pleasant shade,
 The swift-growing China Tree.

Not the spreading beech, 'twill uproot the grass,
Not the oak that allows no sun to pass
 When dark winter days must be.
Cedar nor pine, for they both will wear
Such seedy coats through the closing year;
 Choose the cheerful China Tree.

Now the house is built, two years are flown,
And to stately height has the sapling grown,
 Green feathery tufts bears he;
With spring we hear murmuring of the bees,
They busily hum as sweets they seize
 From the honey-bloomed China Tree.

Then come baby Bessie and maiden May
Beneath its cool shade on the grass to play,
   Now each has a necklace, see;
What need of coral or beads of glass?
When a string through the purple flowers they pass,
   Lilac tubes of the China Tree!

Green berries are here for the bloom is fled,
And that shedding time is the housewife's dread;
   Where can Warren and Thomas be?
A pop gun souds; Don't you hear the noise?
A jolly time you are having my boys,
   Up there in the China Tree.

Sad Autumn now with soft tinted skies,
All her bright hues saved for the woodland dyes;
   Yet with liberal hand doth she
Bring the primrose suit for our friend to wear,
No Gum nor Sumac looks gayer there
   Than this yellow-plumed China Tree.

All have left it at last, even withered leaves,
But the dry brown berry in bunches cleaves
   Where blossoms were wont to be.
And whenever there comes a winter rain,
Over each little ball will a drop remain,
   On the brown-berried China Tree.

They shine in the sun and he colors them, too,
With rainbow tints, as his rays pierce through;
   'Tis a glorious sight to see.
It is time to rest, with your year's work done,
So sparkle you may, in the winter sun,
   Oh, jewel-hung China Tree!

OUR MARGARET.

ONE summer morn, from dreamless sleep I
    woke,
In a fair vale where winds the Roanoke,
And sought the field. There early spiders spun
Their gauzy snares, that sparkled in the sun
With dewdrops caught where wanton flies should be,
Which ox-eyed daisies gaily smiled to see.
These, all unlike their English sisters shy,
That greet the dawn with blushing lid and eye
Half-closed, oped wide their pure white rays,
And met the glowing orb with steady gaze.
Upon a rock that offered friendly rest,
Then sitting down, my rustic hat I dressed
With daisies bright, and plucking, idly thought
Of Goethe's Marguerite; soon fancy brought
Visions of women who have borne that name,
Whose praise still lingers on the lips of fame.
At ancient Antioch, see, in dungeon cast
A Roman maid. "Deny this Christ!" they cry,
"Recant! Recant! Adore the gods, or die!"
"Then welcome Death!" She glories in the flame,
And legends say this flower received her name.

Years roll away; now, wrecked on Scotia's shore,
An English bark. The Saxon hope it bore;
For friendly Fate the Atheling's sister leads
To Malcolm's arms, and sows, through her, the seeds
Of Christian lore amid these mountains wild.
In Norway next, I see Valdemar's child

Three kingdoms join.   Alas! twas all in vain
Your noble work, great Daughter of the Dane!
Wearing a sweet rose stained with bloody strife,
Poor guiltless flower! comes Henry's warrior wife.
The struggling Church seeks shelter in Navarre
With Francis' sister, Angoulême's bright star,
And free Italia, 'mid her vineyards green,
Bows loyally to Humbert's lovely queen.
Thus, one by one, the shadows come and go,
As memory moves the mirror to and fro.
Wearied at length of courtly pomp and pride,
"Now bear me home," to Fantasy I cried.
"There, well I know, some dainty Marguerites
          dwell,
Pure pearls, that all these radiant gems excel!"
Smiling, she led me to my own sweet South,
Where Miche Sepe seeks, through many a month,
The Atlantic sea.

There a fair city lies,
'Mid orange groves, beneath the sunniest skies.
I saw one moving through the bustling street,
A form each passer gladly paused to greet.
No crown she wore, no aureole of saint
Shone round her head, no artist sought to paint
That homely face.   Her simple words declared
No mental worth, nor flash of wit appeared.
What then, her charm?   What this strange woman's
          spell?   .
The needy know, the orphan child can tell.
Of lowly birth, still truest lady she,
In Saxon style, and all humanity
Her household was, for loaves she gave to all.
The poor and suffering never yet did call

In vain to her.   The struggling parish church;
The widow's friend; those who, to succor, search
The homes of want; they who their pure lives spend
Soothing the sick, or gently rear or tend
The motherless; all sought this woman's aid.
She gave them bread, for 'twas by bread she made
The means to live, and these poor brethren raise.
Woman of wealth, a worker all her days!

I looked again, that form no more appeared;
But, in the city's midst, I saw, upreared,
A sculptured stone and that strange marble bore
No hero's form, but seated as of yore
Knitting in hand, a leaning orphan near,
Margaret the Good seems ever smiling there.

———)(———

.

THE ANGEL OF GETHSEMANE.

LUKE 22: 43.

THY glory great as Gabriel's, when, from
    heaven, he bore
The wondrous tidings of a Saviour's birth,
Or princely Michael's, who, in conflict sore,
    Met and o'ercame the Enemy of earth;
Called to convey, thou blest, unnamed one,
The Father's message to the suffering Son!

Be a like mission mine, to seek some heart
    In its Gethsemane of sin and shame
When heaven seems lost, when friends and fame
      depart,
    Then, whispering peace, hope, pardon, in the
      Name
Of One who drank that cup, e'en from the brim,
So cheer His own, as thou didst strengthen Him!

FOR MY DEAR LOVE.

AN OPAL.

FOR my dear love I long to bring,
   Some rare and dainty offering;
I'll steal a rainbow from the sky,
To paint my joy when she is nigh;
The fairness of her form to sing,
I'll mount me on a poet's wing;
Through winter frost, each flower of spring
Shall speak and tell her how I sigh
      For my dear love.

Nay, nay, this is but loitering;
See, here, a tiny rounded thing,
Where all sweet shades imprisoned lie,
Her blush, the flowers, the rainbow sky
Now, I will set this in a ring,
      For my dear love.

SUB ROSA.

I WILL tell you of something that no one knows;
  Of something that happened under the rose.
A gay little bird lighted there one day,
And sang, full of love, a roundelay;
And a bud just peeped from its sheath of green,
To listen and wonder what this might mean.

" When he comes again, in the twilight dim,"
Said the bud, " I will open my heart to him."
So it shook its petals apart and blushed,
Till each crumpled fold to the center flushed,
And sweet perfume whispered of what might be
When the bud was blown from its calyx free.

But the bird came not; there were fairer flowers,
And buds in plenty more rare than ours,
And, ere the sun on the dewdrops shone,
She lay drooping and dead, a bud half blown,
That might never its perfumed heart disclose!
I have told you what happened under the rose.

A MISTAKE.

BECAUSE I knew she loved me,
  And 'twas so sweet to see those wistful
    eyes,
Half-veiled to hide their secret from surprise,
Aside I turned, and, with a courteous care,
Concealed the truth from her I held most dear,
  Because I knew she loved me.

I know she must have loved me!
Yet, when at last, my passion all confessed,
I sought to strain the dear one to my breast,
"Nay, nay," she smiling, said: "too late, too
    late,"
Then showed another's ring. Ah, cruel fate!
  And yet, I know she loved me.

THE LOST MAGNIFICAT.

"I HEARD not Our Lady's song, to-night."
    In sad reproach, the vision spoke,
And the blissful dream of the chorister broke,
Who joyed at the heavenly sight.

'Twas in an abbey of ancient day,
    Where the pious monks in their simple way,
Would at Angelus often sing,
    The Magnificat, that glorious hymn.
    Sweet would it sound through the cloister dim
And amid the old arches ring.

It chanced one day that a stranger came
    Journeying by from some town of fame;
A skilled musician was he,
    With voice well-trained high notes to trill,
    And the deepest tones of the bass to fill,
Sure ne'er was such melody!

Our pious monks had no envy; they
    To each other said, in their simple way,
"Ah, now for once, our favorite hymn,
    Shall be fitly sung."   So they seek the guest
    And gladly he grants, as they request,
Then, when twilight gathered dim,

He led them in the Magnificat,
    With a well-trained voice—Remember that!—
And each note gave cadence true.

But his thoughts! "How these rustic folk do
    stare,
Such singing to them may be something rare,
I must show them what I can do."

Now other singers in awe are still,
For that wonderful voice seems the space to fill.
Yet the words!—Not one they hear.
    He sings, they listen, with one accord,
    But no spirit "doth magnify the Lord."
No sound soars to Heaven's high Ear.

Father Francis hastened into his cell
Alone on the wondrous strains to dwell,
For song was his soul's delight.
    When, sudden, the chamber dark and still,
    Some presence seemed to enter and fill
With a radiance clear and bright.

He bowed his head; "had the Mother heard,
And a message of special grace conferred
So soon by an Angel sent?"
    Ah! no; for sad spake the vision bright,
    "I heard not Our Lady's song, to-night,
For sweet at the sun's descent.

When your hearts in their humble tribute blend,
Each eve that hymn doth to heaven ascend;
Yet pride would retard its flight.
    Your stranger guest, he sang loud and well,
    But each soaring note ever earthward fell,
So we heard not your song to-night."

Then glad and thankful each after day,
Our monks sang their hymns in the same old way,
Though no wonderful voice was there,
    Through the treble and bass to quaver and trill;
    Their grateful hearts could the measure fill,
Make it meet for the Master's ear.

THE WINNING WAY.

"I WILL conquer this iron!" the sharp axe said,
   And with whack, whack, whack,
Gave blow after blow that fell heavy as lead;
But the bar of iron lay cold, black and dead,
Seeming never the worse for the sturdiest hack.
And the edge of the axe at last grew so blunt,
That he gave up the strife with a weary grunt.

"Now leave it to me!" his bright neighbor cried,
   And with saw, saw, saw,
He moved backward and forward from side to side;
Ah! never so well had his temper been tried,
For the motionless iron would show not a flaw.
But its tormentor's teeth, soon grew broken and
      worn,
And, "I fear 'tis in vain," he exclaimed with a
      groan.

"Make way," said the hammer, "Let me give a
      knock!"
With a Ha! Ha! He!
But he lost his head at the very first shock,
It flew off and lodged in an old wooden block,
For the iron was too hard for that, you must see.
When the three stood aside and were blushing for
      shame,
"Will you please let me try," said the gentle flame.

With a scornful laugh, they all gave her place,
And she curled, curled, curled,
Round the hard black bar, with a fiery grace,
'Till it melted and glowed in the soft warm embrace;
Just as cold hearts are conquered by love in the
world.
And the callous and dull oft' by courtesy we gain,
When the unkind and rude all have striven in vain.

PHARAOH'S DAUGHTER.

"Take this child and nurse it for me, and I will give thee thy wages."

QUEENLY daughter of the Nile,
　At whose changing frown or smile,
　　Thousands joy or fear;
Dost thou gaze with pity mild
On the outcast Hebrew child,
　　On the orphan's tear?

Vain the monarchs of thy race
Strive with pyramids to grace
　　Future rolls of fame.
More than all their works of art,
In this deed thy woman's heart
　　Hath embalmed thy name.

Daughters of a Christian land,
Outcast babes on every hand,
　　Look around and see;
Shall, while thus a heathen shows
Pity for an infant's woes,
　　Thou unmovéd be?

Colder than the Nilus wave,
Drearer than a wat'ry grave,
　　Earth with evil dark;
Many human monsters vile,
Fiercer than the crocodile,
　　Wait each little bark.

Idlers in a fruitful land,
Will ye in the market stand,
　　Waiting to be hired?
Are ye not already bought?
Christ for you the conflict fought,
　　On the tree expired.

Come, if at the eleventh hour,
Ere your life, as faded flower,
　　Sees its setting sun.
What though others long have wrought!
Rich reward your work hath brought,
　　So it well be done.

Hast thou money?　Wages give,
So through others they may live
　　Free from tempting need.
Art thou poor?　A word, a smile,
Give your time—a little while
　　Sows eternal seed.

Then, at the great reck'ning day,
Shall the loving Savior say
　　Gracious words to thee;
"As ye all these works have done,
Fed and clothed each little one,
　　It was unto me."

LIZZIE'S PICTURE.

(E. A. B. AGED 2 YEARS).

LIZZIE'S photograph they've brought me,
　Likeness surely hard to trace!
How could any golden sunlight
　Picture such a pearly face?
I've no artist's glowing palette
　Nor the sculptor's chisel rare;
Yet with hues that love hath lent me
　I will paint your portrait, dear.

First the brow, pure as a snowdrop
　Blooming after April rain,
But, replacing verdant touches,
　Here and there a violet stain,
Then the cheeks like velvet rose leaves,
　White like Easter-lily's bell,
Save where dainty little flushes
　Baby joys and sorrows tell.

Sweet mouth pursed, a bud just opening
　To be kissed into the flower;
Parted then its smiles disclosing
　Jewels fit for queenly dower.
Hair that caught its gleam from morning
　Or the gladsome harvest moon,
Fine as though 'twere just unravelled
　From some dainty spun cocoon,

Eyes above whose dreamy azure,
　Snowy lids now softly creep,—
Auntie was too slow and prosy
　Baby Lizzie's fast asleep!

THE RIDE.

TOSS proudly your head, my beautiful bay,
   And canter carefully o'er the rough way,
  For fair is the lady that rides you;
Fair is her face, though dark is her eye
And dark, too, her hair as the dim midnight sky,
  But fair are the fingers that guide you!

Does she know when she strokes you, my beautiful
     bay,
When she touches your mane in that exquisite way,
  How my heart with envy is throbbing?
That, while o'er these lovely meadows I ride
Through sunshine and shadow so close to her side,
  All my peace of mind she is robbing?

She says that she loves you, my beautiful bay,
That you bear her so carefully o'er the rough way
  And answer so well when she guides you;
Oh! what would she say if I told her that I,
Would as willingly yield to be guided by
  The fair little lady that rides you!

MICHAELMAS.

" To the pure heart every home is a Bethel, and every path of
life a Penuel, and a Mahanaim."   REV. F. W. FARRAR.

M ORN early morn! From every home around
    Comes cheerful echo; yet no answering sound
Heard from the village church,
    No organ peal, no hymn to greet the day;
'Till on the tower, we see a bird alight
There, resting from his flight
    Beside the cross, he sings a matin lay.

A small gray bird, dim as the dawn in hue,
Embodied air; Air breathing through and through
Each dainty plumed quill,
    And as he sings, forth from that slender throat
The voices of the wind, all, seem to flow
In cadence soft and low,
    Or in a quaver shrill, or lingering note.

"Venite," "Te Deum," how shall we word the lay?
We praise Thee, Lord, as angels do alway;
'Tis done; "Amen!" "Amen!" "Amen!"
    Tracing that flight amid the encircling blue
We still soar on, in thought, and pierce the skies
'Till to our longing eyes,
    Visions of winged things seen wafted through.

Visions like those to the Apostle shown;
The six-winged seraphim around the throne,
The creatures mid the wheels,

The princely Michael, and his warriors bright,
And Gabriel, with those whose bléssed place
Is near the Father's face,
　　Because Christ's little ones they guide aright.

"I am thy fellow servant, worship God,"
We heed that warning in the sacred word,
Yet on this chosen day.
　　Would search the record of your blest employ,
Ye shining guardians, who befriend us still;
Working the Maker's will;
　　E'en since the hour ye hailed with shouts of joy.

This new-made world.　Angels how oft appear
To Abraham, Jacob—Lot would loiter near
Sodom's accursed plain,
　　They seize his hand and draw him from the doom;
They, in the wilderness, sad Hagar cheer
And show her water near;
　　And when Elijah sleeps o'ercome with gloom;

One brings him food, standing in Baalim's path,
An angel with drawn sword proclaims God's wrath,
Because he goes to curse,
　　The chosen race.　But, gladlier from on high,
To serve the Incarnate One ye did descend
And all His ways attend;
　　No ladder needed then 'twixt earth and sky!

And is the vision sealed ? Nay, grown more near!
Unto the pure in heart, will still appear
God's angels here below,

Where Love, Hope, Faith, abide, they smiling
    stand
They take no outward form yet such may feel
That presence o'er them steal;
    The hosts of heaven are, here, on every hand.

As in Samaria, when the prophet prayed;
His fearful follower by that prayer was made,
With open eyes to see,
    God's chariots encompassed them around,—
An angel struggles with each thought of ill
And heaven re-echoes still
    Whene'er a wandering soul the path has found.

"THE WITNESS OF NINEVEH."

"So the people of Nineveh believed God and proclaimed a fast."—JONAH 3-5.

"The men of Nineveh shall rise in judgment with this generation and shall condemn it."—ST. MATTHEW 12-40.

IN Pul's great city there is feasting.
  For now the mighty king puts by his state;
Beloved of Bel, True son of Nin the Great,
His royal crown and sceptre laid aside,
He sits amond his lords, the nation's pride.
All garlanded with wreaths of fairest flowers,
In song and wine they pass the careless hours.

All through the city there is feasting.
The gods around in bronze and ivory gleam,
No word have they to break the festive dream.
To guard the gate, the winged lions stand,
No incense offered there by pious hand,
No hymns of praise the sacred symbols greet,
And lust and crime run riot in the street.

"Yet forty days and Nineveh shall fall!"
What harsh note mars their sweetest song?
What man is this that breaks through that gay
        throng?
Shrieking his fearful burden on before,
" Yet forty days and all shall be no more,
Thus speaks the great Jehovah, God most high,
A ruined heap, proud Nineveh shall lie."

Now, all through the great city there is mourning,
Thus spake the king, for God had moved his heart,
" Let every soul withdraw himself apart,
For all have sinned.   We, lifted up with pride,
Our Gods their worship due have long denied;
And, most of all, do they abhor the proud;
Now mourn, and weep, and cry to them aloud.

"Cry, too, unto the Hebrew God, for he
Is great.   He led his people through the sea,
Have we not heard?   And how he overthrew
Great kingdoms; how their enemies he slew?
Yet he is merciful, he loveth not to curse.
Haste now, to him your penitence rehearse,
Call humbly on the Gods and mostly cry,
Have mercy, Great Jehovah, God most high!"

In each street of the great city there is mourning,
Not men alone, but beasts must sack-cloth wear.
And ashes now, not roses deck the hair;
No wine they take nor dainty food, scarce bread
May any eat, for so the king has said.
And king, and lords, and people join to cry,
"Have mercy, Great Jehovah, God most high!"

In each home of the great city there is mourning.
The children ask, " How long before that day
That dreadful time, we heard the Hebrew say,
Our city should be but a ruined heap?"
"Soon! soon!" reply the mothers as they weep,
Ye helpless babes, come lend your voices, cry,
"Have mercy, Great Jehovah, God most high!"

Now in Pul's city there is gladness.
'Tis come, 'tis passed, that dreaded, dreadful day!
Their prayer is heard, God's wrath is turned away.
And, while in grateful worship they rejoice,
The angry prophet hears, far off that Voice,
"Thou pitiest a weak gourd thou didst not rear,
Then shall not I this glorious city spare?"

SEA-SHORE CAMP-MEETING.

THE days since you left, dear Zuleika,
   So slowly and sadly had passed,
That I sighed for a change, when, eureka!
   It came with the preacher, at last.

Not that youngster, tall and ungainly,
   Who was on this circuit last year,
Whose watery eyes strove, so vainly,
   To extinguish the glow of his hair.

But a neat, little elderly person,
   And though prematurely I grant,
My heart sprang to brother McPherson,
   When he spoke of camp-meeting to Aunt.

Peggie Jones went the Sunday before,
   The Smiths must be then on the way,
And we both never ceased to implore,
   'Till she promised to start the next day.

So I smoothed out my pink muslin gown,
   And looped it up, this way and that,
And twisted my ancient sundown,
   Into quite an *a la mode* hat.

The sun was just over the trees,
   All aglow for his diurnal round,
When we felt the first kiss of the breeze,
   And saw the blue waves of the Sound.

In a grove where green branches obstructed
　　The ardor of midsummer rays,
Were the tents--neat cabins constructed
　　On the model of Mr. Carré's.

The chapel, a shed in the centre,
　　Supported by numerous posts,
A bugle now called us to enter,
　　With sounds that might waken the ghosts.

Here were hundreds of people collected,
　　From the City, the Bay, and the Pass;
And to many a stare was subjected,
　　Your poor little piney woods lass.

The singing, my dear, was just splendid!
　　Not a choir with opera airs,
Each voice with the melody blended,
　　And then came the longest of prayers.

We prayed for the hardened, the contrite,
　　The wounded, the sick, and the sore;
And that, vilest of all, might be pardoned,
　　The sinners along the seashore.

Then a brother stood up to exhort us,
　　I heard not his place or his name,
But I know the blest truths that he taught us
　　From the holy book certainly came.

His topic was "Self-Consecration,"
　　Of forsaking the pleasures of life,
And I thought, ere he paused, my vocation,
　　Was to be a poor minister's wife.

Just then, through the crowd, what should greet
    me,
  But the glance of a clear hazel eye!
And I knew who had come there to meet me,
  That my own Johnny Thompson was nigh.

Oh! long, at the noon, did we linger
  In the shade near the mineral spring,
'Twas there he placed on my finger,
  This dear little emerald ring.

And I thought that night, ere I slumbered,
  Perhaps as a true, loving wife,
I might with the chosen be numbered,
  Although not a martyr for life.

But sleep overcame me ere seeming
  This question, so hard, to decide,
And I wakened next morning while dreaming
  That *you* were the minister's bride.

IN MEMORIAM.

REV. ALEXANDER MARKS, AUGUST 28th, 1886.

"HE sleeps," some said with sighs,
    Watching in those dear eyes
The light of earth grow dim;
Yet, while the word they spoke,
That soul to glory woke.
    No darkness, now, for him.

At rest, so cold and calm,
Hands folded palm to palm.
    Alas, ne'er, ne'er again,
Our own shall feel their clasp,
The firm, the friendly grasp!
    Hush! hear that other strain;

"We rest not night nor day,
But work His will alway,
    Angels and spirits blest;
No weariness nor care;
No pain can enter here;
    What need have we for rest?"

"Adieu," on earth, was heard
From hearts with anguish stirred.
    In Paradise, was sung
"Welcome, thou soldier true,
See place prepared for you
    The white-robed throng among!

"Faithful in every trust,
Thy armor shows no rust,
  But beareth many a trace
That thou the cross didst share,
The thorny crown didst wear,
  Come, now, His joy embrace!"

*   *   *   *   *   *

Blue mountains that he loved!   Each misty peak
  And grove just tinged with autumn's early glow!
Point heavenward, to his sorrowing loved ones
    speak
  Of peace that passeth all things here below!

And harps are heard, the trumps' triumphant sound,
As ope the gates before the victor crowned;
The rapture, there, no earthly tongue may tell,
Faith sees and hears, then murmurs, "All is well."

WADE HAMPTON'S DREAM.

"I believe, as confidently as I do that I live, that the prayers
of the people saved my life. I will tell you why—"

BLEST is the memory of the dead
   Who for his fellowmen hath bled;
  Greater the hero, when
Crushed by a weary weight of woe,
He still will heavenly rest forego,
  And *live* for other men.

    *   *   *   *   *   *

Fierce fever throbbing through my veins,
The body racked with cruel pains,
  The mind with sense of loss;
I thought: Why longer seek to live?
What can the fairest future give
  To lighten such a cross?

List to the words that met my ears;
"Live, General, for you people's prayers
  Are rising night and day;
In every home throughout the State,
The young, the old, the low, the great,
  For Hampton hourly pray."

My sister, standing near my bed,
The faithful pastor's words had read;
  Now kneeling by my side—
"Oh! brother, hear and rouse your will;
Some earthly mission waits you still,"
  With eager love she cried.

WADE HAMPTON'S DREAM.

I slept, and in the shadowy land
Of midnight dreams soon seemed to stand
   Within a spacious room:
There saw each district of the State;
Old Beaufort, where I dwelt of late,
   Gleamed clearest through the gloom.

Then, from the throng, one person grave
Drew near to me; a touch he gave,
   And said: " These pray for you,
Soldier and statesman, live, live, live! "
His words seemed quickening power to give,
   I woke, as born anew.

The life-blood, creeping through my veins,
Gave strength to meet the cruel pains.
   Now, by God's grace, who hears,
Live for these friends, I will, I will!
Live for the cause of freedom still,
   Saved through my people's prayers.

TARDY.

WE strolled through the autumn woods alone,
    I was fair eighteen, you thirty-eight;
The summer birds had all southward flown,
    For the coming of Love is sometimes late.

I plucked from the frost-touched bough o'erhead
    A golden leaf in my hair to twine;
" Nay, that is the wreath for me," you said,
    "Spring flowers for sunny locks like thine."

I kept that leaf which now seemed dear,
    (The coming of Love is not always late),
It was emblem of one, not "dry and sere,"
    But wise and gifted and good and great.

Yet you gave no sign till hope had fled
    And another came less slow to woo—
Blithe, bonnie and brave. We were quickly wed
    I was then nineteen, he twenty-two.

Your note, received on my bridal morn,
    Said this—(Ah, me! how hard is fate!)—
"At last, sweet one, I have risked your scorn."
    At last, faint heart! Too late, too late!

DISSECTION.

AS man grows callous on the battle field,
   So, when—that nature's law be clear revealed,
A corpse, late all aglow with vigorous life,
Comes to be carved by cold dissecting knife,
One loses soon the unnerving sense of awe.
Yet, at our school a subject once I saw,
The hand of veteran surgeon might have stayed.
I think that evening we were, all, afraid.

Five at my table for position drew;
The head fell mine, its cover off I threw.
We saw a girl, a maid scarce seventeen
Dead but a week, no more, and fair and clean.
Her bonnie hair braided each side came down,
Tied with blue ribbon, locks of golden brown.
Her soft skin all unmarred.   So had the grave,
And ghoul's-hook sought that purity to save.

Moving with care the silken band that bound
Her slender throat, a locket there I found.
A woman's face was pictured in one lid,
Sweet, motherly, with eyes that seeming chid;
The other held strange words for one so mild,—
"God do with them as they with thee my child;
—Mother." The locket back we laid,
And left that corpse untouched.   We were afraid!

THE SILENT BELL.

A LEGEND OF COLOGNE.

IN the Fatherland stands a stately shrine,
  On the storied banks of the lovely Rhine,
    In Cologne, ancient town;
Five-hundred feet do its towers rise,
And, from marble towers that pierce the skies,
    The sculptured saints look down.

Look calmly down on the roofs below,
On the men that are hurrying to and fro,
    Like grains of the desert sand
By warm winds stirred, so small they seem,
Beneath the shade of that poet's dream
    That was sketched by a master-hand.

A dream of heaven, there, framed in stone,
Through the toiling years to its fullness grown,
    Yet, wrought from one wondrous plan,
And each pointed arch, as it seems to blend
With the peaceful sky, bids the soul ascend
    Far, far from the haunts of man.

'Tis a link that binds with the ages past
That Gothic pile, so grand, so vast;
    For, begun with the fifth Crusade,
Not till five centuries had flown,
O'er cable came: "The final stone
    In the spacious dome is laid."

"Now, from these towers," quoth the Germans
    proud,
A mighty bell shall proclaim aloud
    Our noble Emperor's fame;
So, quick in the furnace let us throw,
The guns of bronze taken years ago,
    When we put proud France to shame!"

The workmen framed a monstrous mould,
Full fifty-thousand pounds, we are told,
    Were wrought in that giant bell;
And forth from the flames came a wondrous sight,
A giant in size, but of strength so slight,
    It at once into fragments fell.

One more they cast, and this stands the test,
So heaven they think has the labor blest,
    And 'tis hung in the holy tower.
Now, now must the Emperor's praise be rung—
So, to wake the tones of that iron tongue
    Strive three-score men of power.

It moves at length, but no sound is stirred,
From the giant bell no voice is heard.
    Again, and again they try.
Once, only once, as they labor so,
There wakens a murmur, deep and low,
    A groan or a plaintive sigh.

The "Silent Bell," as 'twas called that day,
To those who beneath it meet to pray,
    This voiceless message bears—
In no temple raised to the Heavenly King,
Should a peal of praise and glory ring
    For the highest of earthly peers.

Lord, cleanse Thy Church as Thou did'st of old,
Cast from it all that is bought and sold;
    To Thy servant who worketh well,
Grant, to give the glory alone to Thee,
Lest his greatest gift should a failure be,
    Like the Emperor's Silent Bell.

———)(———

MUSIC.

DAUGHTER of God, or Belial's slave, she stands
    With fading fillet bound or crowned with stars;
And every soul, as Music soft commands,
    Soars or descends, vaulting all earthly bars.

———)(———

www.ingramcontent.com/pod-product-compliance
Lightning Source LLC
Chambersburg PA
CBHW030551270326
41927CB00008B/1599